"Climb 'Til Your Dream Comes True"

Comes True

A COLLECTION
OF
INSPIRATIONAL
VERSES

by

Helen Steiner Rice

INCLUDING THOSE FEATURED
ON THE LAWRENCE WELK SHOW
BY *Aladdin*

FIRST EDITION
Published
by
GIBSON GREETING CARDS, INC.
1964

FOREWORD

Show me the way,
*   not to fortune and fame,*
Not how to win laurels
*   or praise for my name —*
But Show Me The Way
*   to spread "The Great Story"*
That "Thine is The Kingdom
*   and Power and Glory."*

— Helen Steiner Rice

REMEMBER THIS!

*Great is the power
of might and mind,
But Only Love
Can Make Us Kind...
and all we are
or hope to be
is empty pride
and vanity...
if love is not
a part of all,
The Greatest Man
Is Very Small!*

Contents

"Climb 'Til Your Dream Comes True"

*O*ften your tasks will be many,
And more than you think you can do...
Often the road will be rugged
And the hills insurmountable, too...
But always remember,
the hills ahead
Are never as steep as they seem,
And with *Faith* in your heart
start upward
And climb 'til you reach your dream,
For nothing in life that is worthy
Is ever too hard to achieve
If you have the courage to try it
And you have the *Faith* to believe...
For *Faith* is a force that is greater
Than knowledge or power
or skill
And many defeats turn to triumph
If you trust in God's wisdom and will...
For Faith is a mover of mountains,
There's nothing that God cannot do,
So start out today
with Faith in your heart
And *"Climb 'Til Your Dream Comes True"*!

II

"Seek Ye First The Kingdom of God"

Life is a mixture
            of sunshine and rain,
Good things and bad things,
            pleasure and pain,
We can't have all sunshine,
            but it's certainly true
There is never a cloud
            the sun doesn't shine through . . .
So always remember
            that whatever betide you
The power of God
            is always beside you,
And if friends disappoint you
            and plans go astray
And nothing works out
            in just the right way,
And you feel you have failed
            in achieving your goal,
And that life wrongly placed you
            in an unfitting role . . .

II

Take heart and "stand tall"
        and think who you are,
For God is your Father
        and no one can bar
Or keep you from reaching
        your desired success,
Or withhold the joy
        that is yours to possess...
For with God on your side
        it matters not who
Is working to keep
        life's good things from you,
For you need nothing more
        than God's guidance and love
To insure you the things
        that you're most worthy of...
So trust in His wisdom
        and follow His ways,
And be not concerned
        with the world's empty praise,
But *Seek First His Kingdom*
        and you will possess
The world's greatest riches
        which is true happiness.

III
Ideals Are Like Stars

*I*n this world of casual carelessness
it's discouraging to try
To keep our morals and standards
and our *Ideals High* ...
We are ridiculed and laughed at
by the smart sophisticate
Who proclaims in brittle banter
that such things are
out of date ...
But no life is worth the living
unless it's built on truth,
And we lay our life's foundation
in the golden years of youth ...
So allow no one to stop you
or hinder you from laying
A firm and strong foundation
made of *Faith and Love
and Praying* ...
And remember that *Ideals*
are like *Stars Up In The Sky*,
You can never really reach them,
hanging in the heavens high ...

III

But like the mighty mariner
who sailed the storm-tossed sea,
And used the *Stars To Chart
His Course*
with skill and certainty,
You too can *Chart Your Course in Life*
With *High Ideals and Love*,
For *High Ideals are like the Stars*
that light the sky above...
You cannot ever
reach them,
but Lift Your Heart Up High
And your *Life* will be as *Shining*
as the *Stars Up In The Sky.*

IV

A Graduate's Prayer

Father, I have knowledge,
                    so will *You* show me now
How to use it wisely
                    and find a way somehow
To make the world I live in
                    a little better place,
And make life with its problems
                    a bit easier to face...
Grant me faith and courage
                    and put purpose in my days,
And show me how to serve *Thee*
                    in the most effective ways
So all my education,
                    my knowledge and my skill,
May find their true fulfillment
                    as I learn to do *Thy Will*...
And may I ever be aware
                    in everything I do
That knowledge comes from learning –
                    and wisdom comes from *You*.

V
"Man Cannot Live By Bread Alone"

He lived in a palace
        on a mountain of gold,
Surrounded by riches
        and wealth untold,
Priceless possessions
        and treasures of art,
But he died alone
        of a *"Hungry Heart"*!
For man cannot live
        by bread alone,
No matter what
        he may have or own...
For though he reaches
        his earthly goal
He'll waste away
        with a "starving soul"!
But he who eats
        of *Holy Bread*
Will always find
        his spirit fed,
And even the poorest
        of men can afford
To feast at the table
        prepared by the Lord.

VI

So Swift The Way!
So Short The Day!

*I*n this fast-moving world
        of turmoil and tension,
With problems and troubles,
        too many to mention,
Our days are so crowded
        and our hours are so few,
There's *So Little Time*
        and *So Much To Do*...
We are pressured and pushed
        until we are "dizzy",
There's never a minute
        we're not "crazily busy",
And sometimes we wonder
        as we rush through the day –
Does God Really Want Us
        To Hurry This Way?
Why are we impatient
        and continually vexed,
And often bewildered,
        disturbed and perplexed?

VI

Perhaps we're too busy
                with our own selfish seeking
To hear the dear Lord
                when He's tenderly speaking...
We are working so tensely
                in our self-centered way,
We've no time for listening
                to what God has to say,
And hard as we work,
                at the end of the day
We know in our hearts
                we did not "pay our way"...
But God in His mercy
                looks down on us all,
And though what we've done
                is so pitifully small,
He makes us feel welcome
                to kneel down and pray
For the chance to do better
                as we start a new day,
And life would be better
                if we learned to rely
On our Father in heaven
                without asking "*Why*"...

And if we'd remember
             as we rush through the day,
"The Lord Is Our Shepherd
             and *He'll Lead The Way"*...
So don't rush ahead
             in reckless endeavor,
Remember *"He Leadeth"*
             and *"Time Is Forever"!*

If You Meet God In The Morning, He'll Go With You Through The Day

"The earth is the Lord's
      and the fulness thereof" –
It speaks of His greatness,
      it sings of His love,
And each day at dawning
      I lift my heart high
And raise up my eyes
      to the infinite sky...
I watch the night vanish
      as a new day is born,
And I hear the birds sing
      on the wings of the morn,
I see the dew glisten
      in crystal-like splendor
While God, with a touch
      that is gentle and tender,
Wraps up the night
      and softly tucks it away
And hangs out the sun
      to herald a new day...
And so I give thanks
      and my heart kneels to pray –
"God keep me and guide me
      and go with me today."

VIII

"Flowers Leave Their Fragrance On The Hand That Bestows Them"

There's an old Chinese proverb
    that, if practiced each day,
Would change the whole world
    in a wonderful way –
Its truth is so simple,
    it's so easy to do,
And it works every time
    and successfully, too...
For you can't do a kindness
    without a reward,
Not in silver nor gold
    but in joy from the Lord –
You can't light a candle
    to show others the way
Without feeling the warmth
    of that bright little ray...
And you can't pluck a rose,
    all fragrant with dew,
Without part of its fragrance
    remaining with you.

IX

Heart Gifts

*I*t's not the things that can be bought
that are life's richest treasure,
It's just the little
"heart gifts"
that money cannot measure...
A cheerful smile, a friendly word,
a sympathetic nod
Are priceless little treasures
from the storehouse
of our God ...
They are the things that can't be bought
with silver or with gold,
For thoughtfulness and kindness
and love are never sold ...
They are the priceless things in life
for which no one can pay,
And the giver finds rich recompense
In Giving Them Away.

X

The Key To Living Is Giving!

A very favorite story of mine
Is about *Two Seas in Palestine* –

. . .

One is a sparkling sapphire jewel,
Its waters are clean and clear and cool,
Along its shores the children play
And travelers seek it on their way,
And nature gives so lavishly
Her choicest gems to the *Galilee* . . .
But on to the south the Jordan flows
Into a sea where nothing grows,
No splash of fish, no singing bird,
No children's laughter
is ever heard,
The air hangs heavy all around
And nature shuns this barren ground . . .
Both seas receive the Jordan's flow,
The water is just the same, we know,
But one of the seas, like liquid sun,
Can warm the hearts of everyone,
While farther south another sea
Is dead and dark and miserly –
It takes each drop the Jordan brings
And to each drop it fiercely clings . . .

X

It hoards and holds the Jordan's waves
Until like shackled, captured slaves
The fresh, clear Jordan turns to salt
And dies within the *Dead Sea's* vault...
But the Jordan flows on rapturously
As it enters and leaves the *Galilee*,
For every drop that the Jordan gives
Becomes a laughing wave
that lives —
For the *Galilee* gives back each drop,
Its waters flow and never stop,
And in this laughing, living sea
That takes and gives so generously
We find the way to *Life* and *Living*
Is not in *Keeping*, but in *Giving!*

. . .

Yes, there are *Two Palestinian Seas*
And mankind is fashioned after these!

The Praying Hands

The "Praying Hands" are much, much more
than just a work of art,
They are the "soul's creation"
of a deeply thankful heart –
They are a *Priceless Masterpiece*
that love alone could paint,
And they reveal the selflessness
of an unheralded saint –
These hands so scarred and toilworn,
tell the story of a man
Who sacrificed his talent
in accordance with God's Plan –
For in God's Plan are many things
man cannot understand,
But we must trust God's judgment
and be guided by His Hand –
Sometimes He asks us to give up
our dreams of happiness,
Sometimes we must forego our hopes
of fortune and success –
Not all of us can triumph
or rise to heights of fame,
And many times *What Should Be Ours*,
goes to *Another Name* –

XI

But he who makes a sacrifice,
so another may succeed,
Is indeed a true disciple
of our blessed Saviour's creed –
For when we "give ourselves away"
in sacrifice and love,
We are "laying up rich treasures"
in God's kingdom up above –
And hidden in gnarled, toilworn hands
is the truest *Art of Living*,
Achieved alone by those who've learned
the "*Victory of Giving*" –
For any sacrifice on earth,
made in the dear Lord's name,
Assures the giver of a place
in *Heaven's Hall of Fame* –
And who can say with certainty
Where the Greatest Talent Lies,
Or Who Will Be the Greatest
In Our Heavenly Father's Eyes!

XII

The Windows Of Gold

*T*here is a legend that has often been told
Of the boy who searched for
The Windows Of Gold,
The beautiful windows he saw far away
When he looked in the valley at sunrise each day,
And he yearned to go down
to the valley below
But he lived on a mountain that was
covered with snow
And he knew it would be a difficult trek,
But that was a journey he wanted to make,
So he planned by day and he dreamed by night
Of how he could reach
The Great Shining Light...
And one golden morning when dawn broke through
And the valley sparkled with diamonds of dew
He started to climb down
the mountainside
With *The Windows of Gold* as his goal
and his guide...

XII

He traveled all day and, weary and worn,
With bleeding feet
and clothes that were torn
He entered the peaceful valley town
Just as the golden sun went down
But he seemed to have lost his *"Guiding Light"*,
The windows were dark
that had once been bright,
And hungry and tired and lonely and cold
He cried, *"Won't You Show Me*
The Windows Of Gold?"
And a kind hand touched him and said, *"Behold,*
High On The Mountain Are The Windows Of Gold" –
For the sun going down in a great golden ball
Had burnished the windows
of his cabin so small,
And *The Kingdom Of God* with its
Great Shining Light,
Like the Golden Windows that shone so bright,
Is not a far distant place somewhere,
It's as close to you as a silent prayer –
And your search for God will end and begin
When you look for *Him*
and *Find Him Within.*

XIII

Make This Your Daily Prayer

*B*less me, heavenly Father,
    forgive my erring ways,
Grant me strength to serve *Thee*,
    put purpose in my days . . .
Give me understanding
    enough to make me kind
So I may judge all people
    with my heart and not my mind . . .
And teach me to be patient
    in everything I do,
Content to trust *Your* wisdom
    and to follow after *You* . . .
And help me when I falter
    and hear me when I pray
And receive me in *Thy Kingdom*
    to dwell with *Thee* some day.

MY THANKS!

People everywhere in life
        from every walk and station,
From every town and city
        and every state and nation
Have given me so many things
        intangible and dear,
I couldn't begin to count them all
        or even make them clear...
I only know I owe so much
        to people everywhere
And when I put my thoughts in verse
        it's just a way to share
The musings of a thankful heart,
        a heart much like your own,
For nothing that I think or write
        is mine and mine alone...
So if you found some beauty
        in any word or line,
It's just "Your Soul's Reflection"
        in "Proximity with Mine".